There's A Queen Within

ONEDIA N. GAGE, PH. D.

Her Journey to Building Self—Worth

There is a Queen Within

Her Journey to Building Self—Worth

Her Journey to Building Self—Worth

There is a Queen Within

Her Journey to Building Self—Worth

By

Onedia N. Gage, Ph. D.

Her Journey to Building Self—Worth

Dedication

to all girls

to the girls who showed me that help was important and necessary

to the girls whose path I will cross and who are in need of assistance

to the girls who have survived struggles but needed a life preserver

Nehemiah: The Character Series By Onedia N. Gage, Ph. D.

Nehemiah and His Basketball

Nehemiah and His Big Sister

Nehemiah and His Flag Football Game

Nehemiah and His Football

Nehemiah and His Golf Clubs

Nehemiah and the Bully

Nehemiah and the Busy Day

Nehemiah and the Class Field Trip

Nehemiah and the Hospital Visit

Nehemiah and the Substitute for the Substitute

Nehemiah and the Two Wheels

Nehemiah Found the Mud

Nehemiah Learns to Swim

Nehemiah Reads to Mommy

Nehemiah and the Hot Dog and the Broccoli

Nehemiah Watch Me Add, Subtract, Multiply and Divide

Nehemiah Writes Just Like Mommy

Nehemiah's Family Vacation

Nehemiah's Favorite Teacher Returns to School

Nehemiah's First Day of School

Nehemiah's Sister Moved

Books by Onedia N. Gage, Ph. D.

Are You Ready for 9th Grade . . . Again? A Family's Guide to Success
As We Grow Together Daily Devotional for Expectant Couples
As We Grow Together Prayer Journal for Expectant Couples
As We Grow Together Bible Study: Her Workbook
As We Grow Together Bible Study: His Workbook
The Best 40 Days of My Life: A Journey of Spiritual Renewal
The Blue Print: Poetry for the Soul
From Fat to Fit in 90 Days: A Fitness Journal
From Two to One: The Notebook for the Christian Couple
Hannah's Voice: Powerful Lessons in Prayer
Her Story The Legacy of Her Fight: The Bible Study
Her Story The Legacy of Her Fight: The Devotional
Her Story The Legacy of Her Fight: The Legacy Journal
Her Story The Legacy of Her Fight: Prayers and Journal
I Am.: 90 Days of Powerful Words: Affirmation and Advice for Girls
ILY! A Mother Daughter Relationship Workbook
In Her Own Words: Notebook for the Christian Woman
In Purple Ink: Poetry for the Spirit
Intensive Couples Retreat: Her Workbook
Intensive Couples Retreat: His Workbook
Living A Whole Life: Sermons Which Prompt, Provoke and Provide Life
Love Letters to God from a Teenage Girl
The Measure of a Woman: The Details of Her Soul
The Notebook: For Me, About Me, By Me
The Notebook for the Christian Teen
On This Journey Daily Devotional for Young People
On This Journey Prayer Journal for Young People
On This Journey Prayer Journal for Young People, Vol. 2
One Day More Than We Deserve Prayer Journal for the Growing Christian
Promises, Promises: A Christian Novel
Queen in the Making: 30 Week Bible Study for Teen Girls
Queen in the Making: 30 Week Bible Study for Teen Girls Leader's Guide
She Spoke Volumes . . . And Then Some
Six Months of Solitude: The Sanctity of Singleness Notebook
Six Months of Solitude: The Sanctity of Singleness Prayers and Journal
Tools for These Times: Timely Sermons for Uncertain Times
With An Anointed Voice: The Power of Prayer
Yielded and Submitted: A Woman's Journey for a Life Dedicated to God
Yielded and Submitted: A Woman's Journey for a Life Dedicated to God An Intimate Study
Yielded and Submitted: A Woman's Journey for a Life Dedicated to God Prayers and Journal

Library of Congress

There's a Queen Within:
Her Journey to Building Self—Worth

All Rights Reserved © 2020
Onedia N. Gage, Ph. D.

No part of this of book may be reproduced or transmitted in
Any form or by any means, graphic, electronic, or mechanical,
Including photocopying, recording, taping, or by any
Information storage or retrieval system, without the
Permission in writing from the publisher.

Purple Ink, Inc. Press

For Information:
Purple Ink, Inc.
P O Box 300113
Houston, TX 77230

www.purpleink.net ♦ www.onediagespeaks.com

publish@purpleink.net ♦ onediagage@onediagespeaks.com

ISBN:

978-1-939119-71-1

Printed in the United States

Instructions for use:

This book is designed for you to read the narrative, and use the borders to make notes. Following the notes, there are questions. Answer those thoroughly. Finally, there are projects which you will need to complete.

Grow and share.

Give this all that you are.

And all that you are not.

And everything that you wish that you were.

Dear Queen in Waiting,

I know that it is hard to be a girl. I have survived wanting to kill myself, low self-esteem, low self-belief, sex with boys who did not love me, and a total misunderstanding of my value and worth.

I will tell you that loving yourself is the best achievement you will ever reach. I give you permission to love yourself—regardless of why you don't think that you should.

As you read this note from me, please consider that you have a purpose in this life. I want you to do a few things to see your future for its true worth:

1. Determine what and who is positive versus who/what is negative.
2. Discard the negative. Seriously. You may even feel compelled to tell them that they need to revise how they handle you or they will lose their access in your life.
3. Affirm your positive. If you don't have any, then I can give you some with which to start.
4. Insure that your brain is sexier than your body. I know that society will tell you otherwise, but it is very important that you focus on the exact opposite. We are expected to be beautiful, but we are really dangerous when we are smart as well. With the smarts, your confidence will certainly rise.
5. Decide on a path which gives voice to your goals. Then go for those goals!

There is Queen Inside of you. I hope this book helps you investigate the inner her and affirm her so that she can blossom into the greatness for which you are purposed. Nothing less.

I know that there is a queen inside because there is one inside of me when I would not believe it either. That Queen came out at an appropriate time in my life when I thought life would never get better. But you hold in your hand evidence that purposes unbeknownst to us are developed within us all of the time. This book is the 63rd book I have authored, not counting the ebooks, and Spanish translations, which I am completing.

I am not the statistic I was supposed to be.

Keep focused on the life you are living.

Her Journey to Building Self—Worth

14 | ONEDIA N. GAGE, PH. D.

Dear Advocate, Mentor, Teacher and Parent:

It is hard to talk to and sometimes to reach her. I understand that, however, you must remember a few things. (1) You were once a girl, moody, disliked yourself, and overall, attitudinal; (2) Someone loved you beyond what you deserved; (3) You recovered, survived, and can share some of the worst times of your life so that no one else has to live through similar events. And you can hold your head up. She needs you. And you know it.

So keep the focus. Love her through her remarkable pain and despicable attitude.

Teach her. Because of. In spite of. She is listening, even it she doesn't behave like it.

You need to be fierce, charismatic, authentic, and honest. She is in need of love we all crave from a source which is dependable and trustworthy. She needs you to stand in your place. And do your job.

Yes, it is a hard job but if you weren't supposed to do it, you would not be here doing it. You have tried to resign several times.

Don't quit.

She needs you.

Sometimes you need her.

Be around for her metamorphosis.

If it gets tough, call me. Or email me. I know how hard and horrible it can be. And for what I don't know, we can learn together.

We are one girl away from success!

Because they are worth it!

Onedia N Gage

Onedia N. Gage

Her Journey to Building Self—Worth

Self-Talk for Global Motivation excerpt

By Onedia N. Gage

I believe in me because
in me there's a strength
that makes me strive for
ultimate success derived
from my goals because
there's a hope that I
will overcome my doubts and fears
that I have developed through failures
and rejections for which I have
decided are deficiencies in my character or/and
abilities when in fact those
mistakes stemmed from lack
of information (about that topic)
so after some education I have
made fewer mistakes and become
more intelligent so now I can draw
a new conclusion that
I have to love myself to love others
and I have to forgive myself before
I can forgive others and I have to respect
myself as an independent individual
before I can accept another person
and understand them and I know
I must learn before I can teach and
I have to fail before I succeed

and I need to see and understand before
I can show and share and I have to
be at peace with myself before
I can be at peace with the world
so now I know that believing in
me is true and real and necessary
to continue to radiate the strength
and power that my mind and
body and emotion encompass so that
I then believe in myself that I can
accomplish anything and everything
that I set out to do for myself,
my feminism and my people and my
brothers and sisters of color.

Reprinted from <u>The Blue Print: Poetry for the Soul</u>

Table of Contents

Dedication	7
Letters	13
Poem	17
Girl Defined	21
Girl Developed	29
Vision Statement	39
Mission Statement	43
Leadership	47
Love	53
Role Model/Advocate	61
Education	65
Image	75
Reputation	79
Work Ethic	85
Integrity	91
Challenges/Your Mountains/Your Past	97
Future	107
Appendix of Resources	119
Acknowledgements	135
About the Queen	137

Her Journey to Building Self—Worth

Girl Defined

I am glad to be a girl. I know that you may not always feel that way. Being a girl is hard—difficult at best. Some cultures think and teach that girls are not valuable, should not be educated—because they do not feel that girls are not whole or full citizens, and do not value or respect them.

This world may not embrace you as a girl. However, consider this: we are necessary. Without a girl and a boy, none of us could be created. Secondly, we do not use someone else's definition to define ourselves. The definition of you is based on who you are.

Dictionary.com defines girls as a female child, an unmarried young woman, a daughter, and a sweetheart. While I argue that the definition is basically correct, it is not comprehensive.

As I consider the definition of a girl, I think of me. By the Gage standard, girls are compassionate, smart, loving, nurturing, caring, fierce, outlandish, outrageous, detailed, innovative, thoughtful, focused, kind, considerate, powerful, tenacious, energetic, problem solver, and intuitive. There are other words which describe, and consequently, define girls.

I could add talkative, creative, and considerate.

We are so much more than that limited definition. Quite to the contrary, Gage's definition is closer to our actual definition.

As you develop your definition of yourself, feel free to include any of Gage's definition that you would like.

The only rule for developing your definition is to OMIT ALL of the negative details and adjectives. Omit the negative!

Notes

Notes

Do not continue to keep letting the negative that you feel about yourself, others try to cast upon, or the negative behaviors from your past effect how you define yourself. OMIT the negative!

Use the positive words to reach that idea of yourself.

Smart is okay, acceptable, and now expected. I expect you to give effort to being smart and intelligent. Read. Study. Practice. Memorize. Review. Ask questions. Practice until you understand the work. Practice until you can teach it to someone else.

Be proud of the knowledge and skills you possess. You have the capacity to retain and apply and learn information. You need to maximize that as opportunity to insure that you education supports the future that you desire.

Girls are loving. We love others and expect to be loved in return. When that love is not returned or is conditional, our self-esteem shrinks. The truth is that we need to love more. Unconditionally. Not expecting anything in return. As a girl, you have a life ahead that will have its victories and its challenges. You will need that love to endure those times. Love others more than they deserve. Love like your life depends on that love. Because it does!

Love extravagantly. Love frees your soul. It gives you freedom of spirit. Your love helps others love and empowers them to be themselves—whoever that is.

Girls are fierce about our beliefs. We are fierce when we care about someone. Fierce is simply an energetic focus about a matter or person. Fierce means that we intentionally give ourselves and our energy to someone or something with the expected successful outcome. Fierce means that you give something **all that you have** and **all that you are.**

You may find it hard to comprehend the fierce concept, initially. But consider this: what do you intentionally give all that you are to or something that you truly believe in? The answer to that is when you applied your fierceness. Fierceness parallels commitment.

Girls are smart. We have a unique way of thinking, which leads us to smarts and intelligence. It is okay to be smart. It is necessary to be smart

You are going to need that knowledge—now and later. Without smarts, you will always be at the mercy of someone else for your life and your learning potential. I know that in at least one culture, it is not encouraged to be more intelligent and definitely as smart. When I learned of that, I was so hurt. I could not believe it was true. But I confirmed this with a female student, and her father. I asked his permission with her present for her to be smart. He consented. I saw a new student in her in the classroom.

Commit to your studies. Study the material. Memorize. Retain that information. Apply that information. Do your best in class.

Be okay with being smart. Your smarts are necessary for your life. People discriminate against people who are not smart and are not documentably educated. The job description rarely reads: 'No education required.' That means that education is important. Your education will require some sacrifice. So exert your energy for your education: this has been known to have monetary dividends in the future.

Girls are compassionate and nurturing. We are understanding and listeners. On the contrary, we are viewed as weak. We need our hands held when are walking up the steps. We need men to stand when we come to the table to be seated. We need our doors opened and closed. We are labeled damsels in distress.

All of this is true.

None of that removes our power or influence. Others would like to participate in your definition. They will base that definition on your behavior, including your words, inclusive of the use of foul language, your social media presence, your attire, your grades, and your attitude.

You determine what they are able to say about you by what you do and what you allow them to see. You are in total control of that image. With that being said, then you need to control the image, the words, and the message.

Notes

1. What is your definition of a girl? How did you reach that definition of a girl? How do you measure up to that definition? If you are not close, then why not? What will it take to reach your own definition?

   _____
   _____
   _____
   _____
   _____

2. Who do you compare yourself to? Who do you need to measure up to as a girl?

   _____
   _____
   _____
   _____

3. What does it take to be a great girl? Who is measuring that progress?

   _____
   _____
   _____
   _____

4. What help do you need to be great? Who can help you?

   _____
   _____
   _____

Project

1. Create a mirror.

This mirror will be decorated all over with details of you and your favorite details.

2. Vision Board

Phase 1.

    Photo of you.

Goals for being a great girl.

Goals for Life.

There's A Queen Within

Girl Developed

Notes

How do girls get to be great? Why are some girls considered great and others are not? What makes girls great? What does it cost to be great? Who is responsible for developing great girls? As a girl, what will you do to contribute to your development as a girl?

Girls develop differently than boys; different things are important to each gender. Girls develop at a different rate than boys. Development means that we as girls are nurtured and educated to greatness. There may be a person that helps your development, like a mentor, or an advocate. This person is designed to help you learn, grow and understand what is in store for your life. This development is critical for your competitiveness as a girl in a world which has issues accepting you.

Development includes what others see: physical appearance, attire, education, and social skills. When I consider the definition of great, consider the girls who contribute to the community, earn good grades, invest in herself in all areas, respect all persons, especially herself, and finally, great girls are considerate of others, their feelings, their needs and their thoughts. Great girls also consider the consequences of her actions. In the definition of a great girl, it may sound like she is perfect. That is not true. She is conscientious of her impact on herself, others, and the world.

Great girls look and aspire to be great. They attempt greatness daily. Even when they fail, they start again tomorrow with the next level of greatness. This definition of great girl will evolve over time as well. The definition is not about perfection; it is however, about genuine effort, consistent effort, and commitment to excellence.

First step to greatness: DECIDE to be GREAT! Greatness is a decision. That only you can make. Decide to be awesome, rather than mediocre.

Second step to greatness: NEVER QUIT! Once you decide to be great, you cannot change your course. Don't let anyone get you off the task of being great. Greatness is a journey.

It requires all of your attention. You cannot spend any time on anything other than being great. All efforts need to go toward great. If that 'behavior' does not contribute toward great, then you don't do that 'behavior.'

Development of Greatness

What Others See

Whatever other people see on your body, your clothes, your hair, and, your skin, are all areas where people judge you. Your clothes send a statement about you. Too short. Too tight. Too sheer. Inappropriate based on the environment or occasion. With that in mind, consider the length of your clothes, specifically skirts. Check the blouse's sheer factor by putting your hand in the blouse in front of sunlight or the brightest lights. You want to check your blouse so that you are not embarrassed when someone says that they can see your bra or underwear. The other concern is making sure that you do not wear colors (such as pink or other bright colors) under white garments. These colors can be seen underneath those garments, which invite unwanted attention.

If your clothes are tight, then what message are you sending? Whether fair or not, based on those clothing decisions, you are judged, and possibly discriminated against. Why do they need to be so tight? What's the purpose of that?

I will assure you that as your self-esteem increases, your clothes will fit properly and the length is always appropriate. You no longer need tight clothes or short clothes to attract the attention of anyone.

There are a billion selfies taken daily. Do you really think that you want to live through seeing that image in the future?

Is that fair? Not necessarily, but it happens daily. This one of the reasons that schools have standards for dress. Otherwise, education could be derailed with the wrong skirt length.

Physical Appearance and Attire

Physical appearance is based on what others see. Attire is a determining factor of this matter. Hair. Nails. Face. Piercings. Tattoos. Blemishes. All of the details which are also how you express and judge yourself. Your visual presentation sends a message. Sometimes that presentation is so iconic that you may not be able to desert that presentation. Be careful of what you are known for. Your idea of cool maybe confused with low self-worth, a scared girl, a scarred girl, and disrespectful.

Is it bad to want to express yourself or try new things on yourself? No, but consider the long-term effects.

Some companies—where you may want to work—do not hire people with tattoos and facial piercings. Your self-expression may be labeled as deviant, non-compliant behavior which will not be productive for their organization. Your presentation may not be well received by their customers, so you will not be considered an asset, then your skills and talents will be overlooked and ignored.

This is information some people never benefit from until it is too late to make a different decision.

As you grow and experiment, consider the long-term effects of your decisions. If you continue with tattoos, consider making them non-visible when you would dress for work. Tattoos are such a big deal now that there are tattoos removal services for persons who have changed their minds about the need for them.

Attire

We discussed is some but again, the attire chooses things for you that you have not considered. Attire makes choices for you that you are not aware of.

Choose in a manner that announces that you know the choice that you are making. You need to consider what opinion your attire causes others to form. Do you really want the attention some of that attire brings? You do not know the complete impact of your attire. You never know who is

Notes

watching you or your social media posts. This is a major deciding factor, which you are the sole decision maker. Decide wisely. If you are not sure, always error on the side of caution and avoid that attire. Otherwise, ask for some sound advice. If you do not have anyone, email me for advice. I will gladly share my opinion.

Education

Announcement: It is okay to be smart! It is encouraged that you learn everything that you can, retain everything you learn, and ask every question that comes to mind. If you are not educated, then you will be denied many opportunities, even those for which you feel qualified. Education is used as a discriminatory factor when possible and as necessary.

Maybe your culture does not honor education for girls and/or your family is not as educated. You may feel guilty about being more educated than your family or overstepping your cultural boundaries. Maybe your neighborhood does not have a reputation for being smart or educated. This is a difficult subject to approach and discuss, however, this is very necessary and important. Education offers you an opportunity to change your legacy. If your family is not educated, then BE FIRST!

If your family is educated, then carry on and maybe go farther.

Your education offers you options that you need for a better life. Most job descriptions stipulate that a high school diploma and bachelor's degree are required for consideration for employment. How will you feel if you don't have the qualifications, but are otherwise perfect for the position? This is a very uncomfortable position to be in.

Go to class. Listen. Takes notes. Ask questions. Do your best. Retain information. Remember the lessons. Study. Take your time on your exams. Go to tutorials. Do whatever it takes to be smart. Intelligence is respected, which causes you to respect yourself.

Education is necessary and free, but so often we neglect it to be popular, or at least not teased for being smart. I ask you to strongly consider the converse: what it you are teased for not being smart and you really don't know? My advice and encouragement is that you consider being smart. I am not suggesting that you boast or even tell others, but you will need that knowledge and intelligence for later to be successful and to achieve your dreams and desires.

'I would rather you to have it and not need it than to need it and not have it.' That statement is made hoping that you understand how valuable your education will be, when you least expect it.

Take the opportunity to be educated. Someone sacrifices to educate you. It is free. Some people are more educated than others. Why? All education is not created equally. Some people are really taking it so seriously that they do more than is required. They also do not complain about the education that they are invited to engage. It amazes me that we reject the one thing that is given to us, and at that rejection, we have discriminated against ourselves. So when others want to discriminate against us, we help them to do so.

Education is an investment in yourself. You control that, and only you can stop you from being educated. Don't make it easy to be discriminated against. Greatness is active engagement in your education.

Social Skills

From using the correct fork to understanding how to shake hands, to the importance of a great hand shake. From knowing how to waltz to the proper etiquette when meeting the President of the United States. These are social skills which you need but you may never know when you will actually use those skills.

When initially introduced, it may seem annoying or seem useless. Until you need it. And you look or/and feel ridiculous because you chose to ignore the lessons.

Social skills include knowing to cross your legs at the ankles when your skirt is short. These skills are a grade which lands on several people—the parent/guardian, teachers, mentors, organizational leaders, or whomever paths you have crossed.

Notes

Social skills include the volume you speak in a room. Greatness is progressive. Greatness can happen daily. Greatness is possible, which requires focus. Be great!

Your development requires your involvement.

This includes the appropriate length of your skirt and dress.

1. What is your definition of great?

   _____
   _____
   _____
   _____

2. How do girls get to be great?

   _____
   _____
   _____
   _____

3. Why are some girls considered great and others aren't?

   _____
   _____
   _____
   _____

4. What does it take to be great?

   _____
   _____
   _____
   _____

5. Who is responsible for developing great girls?

___

6. As a girl, what will you do to contribute to your development as a girl?

___

7. What do you have to do to be great by your definition?

___

Project

1. Goals
   - This month
   - This quarter (3 months)
   - Six months
   - This year

2. Letter to yourself about what you want to be when you grow up.

Vision Statement

A vision statement is a declaration of an person or organization's objectives, intended to guide its internal decision making. An aspirational description of what you would like to achieve or accomplish in the mid-term or long-term future. It is intended to serve as a clear guide for choosing current future courses of action. (Source: Wikipedia.)

What is your vision for yourself? What do you want to achieve in life?

If you want to be an attorney, then you have to attend law school. In order to attend law school, you will need an undergraduate degree. In order to earn an undergraduate degree, you need to graduate from high school. In order to graduate from high school, then you need to attend classes daily, do all assignments, and have great behavior.

Your vision stops your attempts to quit. Vision counters the desire to quit. Your vision is more important than escaping the short-term uncomfortable situation as labeled homework and tests.

Vision defeats idle time. Vision directs your behavior away from self-destruction. Vision counteracts lack of productivity. Vision establishes you as a serious person about your life and your future.

The vision statement is what you refer to when you forget what you need to be strong. It does not make you infallible, however, it does decrease the chances to fail.

Notes

1. What do you want to do? List all that you want to do. Do not edit the list based on what people say that you can or cannot do.

   _____
   _____
   _____
   _____
   _____
   _____
   _____
   _____
   _____
   _____
   _____
   _____
   _____

2. What are the possible obstacles of achieving those goals?

   _____
   _____
   _____
   _____
   _____
   _____
   _____
   _____

Project

Vision. Create the statement.

Draft the statement below. In the framed page, write the final version. Mount the final version in several of your spaces (bedroom, closet, bathroom). Take the photo of it and make it your lock screen photo on your phone.

VISION STATEMENT

_____
_____
_____
_____
_____
_____
_____
_____
_____
_____
_____
_____
_____
_____

Mission Statement

There's A Queen Within

Mission statement is a statement of purpose, identifying your values, intent of your life, and how you plan to achieve that.

Essential parts of the mission statement are purpose and goals.

The following questions must be answered in the mission statement, according to Forbes:

1. What do you do?
2. What do you want to do?
3. How do you do it?
4. What is the plan?
5. Whom do you do it for?
6. Who is your audience?
7. Who is the motivating source?
8. Who is the reason you do this?
9. What is your why?
10. What is the value of what you do?
11. What is the benefit of what you do?

The statement works in conjunction with the vision statement to create results. You are created to produce. The two statements work in conjunction to keep you focused and on track for the life you desire and for which you will work hard.

As you grow older and as you achieve some of these goals, these statements will need to be revised.

As you consider your purpose and your why, understand that it will be challenged, mostly by you. These are very important statements which have the power and influence to force you to take the right steps and make the right moves. You will need that from time to time. There will be days when you will plan to do wrong, when you will want to quit doing what is right, and it is then when these statements—these words, individually and collectively—will redirect your course.

Notes

1. What do you do? What do you want to do?

_____
_____
_____
_____

2. How do you do it? What is your plan?

_____
_____
_____
_____

3. Whom do you do it for? Who is your audience? Who is your not quitting source? What is your why? Who is the reason why you do this?

_____
_____
_____
_____

4. What is the value of what you do? What is the benefit of what you do?

_____
_____
_____
_____

Project

1. Mission—Create the Statement.

Draft the statement below. In the framed page, write the final version. Mount the final version in several of your spaces (bedroom, closet, bathroom). Take the photo of it and make it your lock screen photo on your phone.

MISSION STATEMENT

_____
_____
_____
_____
_____
_____
_____
_____
_____
_____
_____
_____
_____
_____

Leadership

You are a leader. You have influence. Even if it does not seem or feel like it. Leadership is about your voice and you only need your own permission to use your voice.

My definition of leadership is that it has nothing to do with ability, but instead your inability to let things fall apart around you.

Do you fix stuff or do you let things fail around you? While that is a personal decision, it is a full reach moment, where you reach out for the people and issues which need to be saved or fixed. It is part of your responsibility to lead when necessary.

That is another leadership quality: rising to the occasion. Meeting the need.

The Leaders You Admire

Who leads around you? Teacher? Parent of a friend? Organizational sponsor? I remember a lady that was part of a teen organization which I was part of—these ladies were awesome. They taught me a lot. What I did not know was I would know them for the rest of my life because I joined two organizations which would connect us for life. Leadership means that you trust your voice and you rise to the occasion.

What else does leadership mean? One is the ability to make change happen with those in need.

Teachers. Parents. Parents of friends. Coaches. Counselors. Principals. These are some of your designated leaders. Are they failing you? Are you they actively leading you?

Are they teaching you? Are they mentoring you? Are they inspiring action within you?

Notes

Leadership:

- Define how you will lead yourself and eventually others.
- Identify someone in leadership whom you admire.
- Let them know that you are watching their leadership.
- Meet with them so that they can help your discover your personal leadership style.
- In addition, they can steer you toward leadership opportunities or steer opportunities toward you.

Is your future, as early as tomorrow, based on what you do today? Leadership is an everyday act where you display who you are. Leadership is not taking over the event or the situation. Leadership also includes being able to follow, when leadership is present and active.

Leadership done well includes enhances self-esteem, and respect for others. The questions become how do you become a leader, when do you become a leader, is it your decision, or do you hope others will invite you to lead, amongst others. When you lead, who will you be? What will you lead? Do you have to be inspired by the cause to lead? Or do you just lead because there is a need? What is your definition of a leader? What does it take to reach that level? Who fits that definition? How do you become your definition of leadership? How can you gain leadership experience?

What leadership skills do you need to develop to be the leader that you can trust?

Leadership also means doing the right thing at all times, putting the needs the others before your own, and keeping your word. Leadership never quits. Leadership means that you remain optimistic in times of trouble. Leadership teaches others to be successful. Leadership helps others when they need uplifting. Leadership helps others when times are tough. Leadership is not selfish. Leadership solves problems in the best interest of the whole group, not one person or one group of people. Leadership does not always have to speak out loud, but seeks the good of all involved.

Leadership seeks the greater good in all circumstances and situations.

1. Define leadership, using your perspective.
   _____
   _____
   _____

2. Who is the leader that you admire? Why? What did she say or do to get your attention?
   _____
   _____
   _____

3. What does leadership mean? How does lack of leadership change your life?
   _____
   _____
   _____

4. When you lead, who are you?
   _____
   _____
   _____

5. What event/people do you what to lead?
   _____
   _____
   _____

6. How does what you do today affect your future?

_____
_____
_____

7. Do you have to be inspired to lead or do you rise to the occasion because there is a need?

_____
_____
_____

8. What is required to be an effective leader?

_____
_____
_____

9. Who fits your definition of a leader?

_____
_____
_____

10. How do you match or become your definition of a leader?

_____
_____
_____

11. How can you gain leadership experience?

_____
_____
_____

12. What leadership skills do you need to develop to be the leader that you can trust?

_____
_____
_____

Project

1. Place pictures of those who lead you and who you admire.

2. Indicate why you admire them and their leadership.

_____   _____
_____   _____

Love

Love is defined as a feeling of warm personal attachments or deep affection, as for a parent, child, or friend. This is love used as a noun. As a verb, love is demonstrated through words and deeds and behavior.

Love has a few definitions, according to the dictionary. However, as it relates to actual people, each of us has our own definition(s). We each measure love differently and with different check points and different tests of another's love. As a teenage girl, you may not know for certain if someone loves you, however, you are absolutely certain when someone does not love you.

I have witnessed young girls question the love of adults around them because of what has happened in their pasts. This testing/questioning, appearing as rejection, is a test of endurance. Your first test is whether the person authentically loves you. Your second test is 'how long will you be here to love me?' Your third test is 'are you like the others who are supposed to love me but actually only use me for their personal gain or satisfaction?' The fourth test is 'what is the benefit of your love to me?'

Based on those four tests, you determine if you are loved so that you can return that love as well. These tests are not announced, sometimes not even planned, but they happen and in no particular order. They are implemented as soon as the adult who needs to be tested presents themselves. Their behavior(s) determines how long the test(s) are administered.

As a teacher, I have told this to young ladies who are testing me. I invite them to continue this practice. Likewise, I give them points to consider as you measure the love which others give you. I will share those with you as well.

I apologize for you having to test the adults that you are supposed to be able to automatically trust. I also apologize that the adults that are supposed to love you have disappointed you or do not appear to love you or are absent. We, teachers, mentors, and leaders, are not trying to replace them. We are support for you regardless of others, inclusive of

Notes

Notes

parents. So consider adults as contributors because of whatever you need at that time.

This love should be unconditional and free. Everything that you have costs you something. Love should not cost you or be based on an exchange for something.

Unconditional love on demonstration is based on what people do for you and the conversations of which you are the recipient. This means that they are investing in you. This is designed to encourage you to continue to invest in yourself.

Love sometimes does not appear like love to you. Let me explain. Love includes the teacher giving you homework. So when the teacher gives you homework, realize that your competition for college, and even for high school, college admittance, college scholarship monies, and National Merit Scholarship Qualifiers are all doing homework. When a teacher does not give homework or does not expect you to do homework, that means that the teacher does not believe that you will do the homework or do not consider that the investment of homework is worth it for you. Either way, that is not love. You measure love by the other person's authentic investment in you. Sometimes it is hard to see, but overall all people that actually love you will unselfishly invest in your life and your future.

Investment means homework, school work, expecting your best, holding you accountable when you need it, motivational talks, as needed, and making sure that you are on track for a life that you can be proud of.

Investment means that they may always be in your face and on your case so that you can remain focused. Investment means that they require that you give your best self to yourself for a productive future. Investment, synonymous for love, means that this person sees potential in you that you are uncertain of at this time.

Love is not abstract. Love is a verb, which means that action is the evidence of that love.

Love also does not cost you anything that is detrimental. So consider carefully why love is important. Ask yourself what does that cost me?

Love also does not include inappropriate relations with adults. They may use 'love' to persuade you that it is okay, however it is not okay at all.

Use this as a rule: If you cannot tell another adult what is happening or what was proposed, then you should not do it AND you should definitely tell the nearest adult.

The difference is a teacher helps you with your homework, then you would be able to share shamelessly. If what might happen causes you shame, then it should not be happening.

Love communicates with you on an honest and authentic level. Love is helpful and healthy. Love is powerful and consistent. The most powerful strength you will ever exercise is to recognize love and honor it. Conversely, when you are able to walk away when you recognize that love is not present, you are maturing. That is a strength you will need for the rest of your life.

Love yourself. No matter what has happened. No matter how you feel about yourself. Forgive yourself so that you can love yourself. This will be a task for the remainder of your life—remember to love yourself. Your self-love is the measure of how people will love you, and respect you.

Your love for yourself will translate to your self-esteem, your self-respect, your self-worth, and how others respond to and treat you. Your self-love will dictate your posture and disposition.

Love is important. To be loved is critical. To love is crucial.

Love.

1. Define love.

_____
_____
_____

2. How did you construct/gather that definition?

_____
_____
_____

3. Who do you love? Why?

_____
_____
_____

4. Who loves you? How do you know?

_____
_____
_____

5. What does it take to love others?

_____
_____
_____

6. What does it take for others to love you?
_____
_____
_____

7. Who wants to love you but you have rejected?
_____
_____
_____

8. Can you fix it? What does it take to accept their love?
_____
_____
_____

9. What does it take for you to trust the adults around you? If so, why? Is it difficult?
_____
_____
_____

10. What does it take for you to love yourself?
_____
_____
_____

11. Who taught you how to love? Who is responsible for your attitude about love? If it is not a good definition, can your definition be repaired?

_____

_____

_____

Project

1. Create a collage of all of those persons who love you.
2. Add to it the people that you want to love you.

3. Write a definition of love you can post which you aspire to practice and embody.

_____
_____
_____
_____
_____
_____

Role Model—Advocate

Your favorite teacher or counselor. The one person who you listen to whenever they speak. The person who gives good advice. The person you admire. So why do admire this person? What do they do that you really like? Why do you respect them? Do you ask them questions about life? What made this person stand out amongst the rest of the people who you know?

Role models are people who lead lives which can be followed. It does not mean that the role model/mentor/advocate is perfect, but it does mean that she/he strives to her/his best to do the right thing as well as helps others to do the same. This person invests in you and holds you accountable for all that you encounter. The advocate helps you reach the goals, which you set for yourself or ones that you set together.

What does the role model/advocate/mentor do? What do you do with a role model/advocate/mentor?

The role model leads by example. She does what she expects of others. The role model is an overcomer. The role model will not be ashamed to share how she overcame the obstacles and difficulties she had to endure to reach the achievement level she desired. The role model teaches you to be an achiever and an overcomer.

The role model is realistic and encouraging, not discounting or criticizing. This role model helps you to develop goals, put dates and action plans to these goals. The role model will put people in your life to help these goals come to fruition, as well. The role model helps to keep you focused and accountable. The role model will require you to work on your own behalf as well.

The mentor asks questions and requires you to think. This is training for the future. This investment is mutual for your growth. You need to grow and stretch yourself so that you will be the person that you desire to be.

Notes

Notes

When you and the mentor started this shared investment in YOUR life, the mentor gave up time that she could have been doing something else for herself or others. Honor the time and commitment by being committed and completing any tasks and assignments between meetings.

The next level depends on this level being successful. You need to take this time very seriously. You also need to realize that she is VOLUNTEERING her time so use it well. Ask questions. Listen. Apply what you learn. Seek to understand what you don't know. Keep watch over your behavior and attitude so that she continues to want to help you. Be honest. Be open to learn. Forgive others who have hurt and harmed you so that you can receive what the mentor is doing for you.

This may take awhile to embrace, understand and put into your daily life but everyone is NOT out to hurt you. There are people who are in your life who have shown up just to help you, expecting NOTHING in return. I know that you may find that difficult to believe, however it is true. Everything that you receive will not cost you in a harmful way.

Your mentor/role model/advocate will also help others view you with the lens that she uses to see you. At this point, she is advocating for you and she is also attempting to overcome your current, less than favorable image. She will try to help you to overcome that "bad girl" image, which you were solely responsible for creating. In this advocacy moment, it is your job to be the person that she says that you will be. This is not the time to assert yourself and forget where we are going. She is asking both of you to put the past in the past. With that being said, you can no longer act as you have previously or you will make her look bad. Her credibility will be reduced because you cannot keep your part of the deal she made on your behalf.

People have peculiar behavior sometimes. This person treats you better because of the involvement of the advocate. Isn't that amazing? So do not ruin your favor with either persons because of a temporary and solvable issue.

Talk. Listen. Share. Be open. Create a great environment with your awesome attitude. Make it pleasant to help you, mentor you, and advocate for you.

1. Do you have a mentor/role model/advocate? Write her/his name and label her/his role(s).

___

2. Who do you go to when you have an issue/trouble?

___

3. Who talks to you when you should be receiving severe consequences?

___

4. Who shares with you rational thinking and correct knowledge?

___

5. Who encourages you to do very best and does not accept your excuses?

___

Project

Write a letter of thanks to someone who has helped you.

Write a letter to your favorite teacher. Thank her/him and share with her/him why she/he is your favorite.

Write a letter to someone you admire.

Education

Education is financially free, but it does cost your time, effort, and energy. The fact that education is free seems to devalue it for some people. If it had a cost associated with it, would people figure out a way to be educated? Similar to material desires, when they cannot afford it, they steal it. If it cost real money, would we treat it differently? Right now not everyone treats education with the importance it deserves.

There are students who do not do homework, class work, tests or even go to class. Is that because it is free or does school not have any value to those individuals? Try this: find someone who does not have a high school diploma. When you find them, ask them do they regret not having one?

Follow up with the following questions:

- Why did you stop going to school?
- Why didn't you ever go back to complete your studies for your diploma?
- Do you regret it now?
- What has not having a diploma stopped you from doing?
- Do you ever consider returning to school for the diploma or a GED?
- What advice do you have for me?

The other person is not going to enjoy this series of questions, and it may be hard for you, however this is a real scenario for all parties involved. The last question could be: 'Would you consider going back now?'

Secondly, ask those same questions to someone who attended college but did not graduate.

Thirdly, for the person who has never attended college, 'why didn't they attend college?'

You need some insight into these matters. Education is the first key to competing in the world that is prepared to discriminate against you because of your gender and then maybe your skin tone or culture or religion/faith or family background.

Of all of those factors, you only control your education. Do not let your lack of education lead to more discrimination, which could be avoided.

Education needs to be respected and regarded and inhaled—greedily. Fiercely ingested. This is your advantage and your competitive edge. Education enables you to compete on the world stage.

School attendance is critical. Absences mean that you miss the instruction. Missing instruction means that you have to figure out what you missed and what you do not know. So when will you learn what you missed while you were out? Go to school. Daily. Even when you don't feel like it. Especially when you do not feel like it.

Be attentive. Pay attention. Follow the school rules. Obey the classroom rules. Be engaged in the lesson. Ask questions when you do not understand. Help others when you do understand. Participate in your education. It's the key to the power and access you will want for the rest of your life. Do your very best when you are there.

Grades are the evidence of work ethic. Work ethic means that you give your best effort at all times, regardless of how you feel about the topic, and regardless of how you feel about school in general.

Give your best effort—at all times. Turn in **all** assignments. When you don't understand the material, then ask questions. Decide to be smart, intelligent, and knowledgeable. All of this leads to success for your school involvement and builds capacity for your life.

Middle school grades follow you to high school. High school grades determine college admittance and acceptance. High school discipline is reported to colleges now as well. High school grade point average (GPA) starts when you start high school, which in some cases is in 8th grade with Algebra 1. Your college grade point average stays with you for the rest of your life.

With this being said, I want to note that your children may ask about your grades and to see your report cards. You want to be proud to share these documents. My daughter asked a former teacher what kind of student I was. The educator was proud to announce the student that I was. Be sure that you are able to share with a particular level of pride.

Education is the difference between you and the next person who wants the same jobs and the same promotions. Education also fuels your self-esteem. The more options that you have, the better you will feel about yourself.

College is when you start making decisions about which make life choices. If you study science, you probably won't be a lawyer. If you study math, you can be an engineer, but not a dentist. College offers you a specialty education which develops into a career of your choice. So as you consider your career decisions, those career decisions determine your college studies and the college that you will attend.

As you progress in your career and education, you will find that some additional opportunities are available if you have more education and more experience. You may find it necessary to get your master's degree in your field or a related field. This will separate you from the competition, setting you apart. Finally, the doctorate degree further separates you because of what it requires.

Set your sights and goals high because you never know what is waiting for you if you are prepared.

Education is your freedom. Give it all that you have.

1. Who encourages you to be educated? Who tells you that it is great to be smart?

_____

_____

2. Why do you have a hard time believing in yourself? What can help you to better believe in your abilities? And to try beyond your perceived abilities?

_____

_____

3. What is your desired career? What education is required to make that a reality?

_____

_____

4. Will you be the first member of your family to graduate from high school? Which college would you like to attend? Graduate from college?

_____

_____

5. What will you do to insure you are as educated as possible? Who will help you?

_____

_____

6. How do you make sure that you do not quit, and finish the course?

_____

_____

Project

1. Research two colleges of your choice. Make a poster of the admittance requirements. Include GPA, SAT/ACT scores, Major(s), Picture of college, Cost(s), and the actual application.

2. Write the college essay which will be required for the application. Ask your high school counselor and English teacher help you to edit the essay. If you are not comfortable with that, then use Grammarly.com.

Image

When people see you, what do they think? What do you wear? Why? What does your hair say about you? Why did you choose that style? What does your image say about you?

Image is based solely on your outward appearance. At this point in your life, some of those choices are yours alone.

As you consider your image as you grow older, what image will you have? Will you be wild or conservative or somewhere in between? Your image translates into how others treat you. Your image dictates how people listen to you and respond to your ideas.

Consider that sheer clothing and tight clothing and short clothing will not be seen as professional and not taken seriously. Also, consider these image details lead people to think that you may be sexually active, which may attract attention that you do not desire and that you may have problems getting away from.

How you dress may be your choice but keep in mind how people respond is their choice, regardless of which of you is right or wrong.

Consider the global view of your life and decide if your lifetime's goals can handle these image decisions.

Candidates for Presidents, Congress and Supreme Court Justices, along with the heads of the FBI, Homeland Security, and other major departments, including CEO's of major companies, endure extensive background checks and investigations. Is your gothic phase or your mean girl phase or your hip hop phase aligned with the future you are destined to fulfill? Don't let your dreams suffer because you were experimenting with a few things.

People will judge you and some are self-authorized to stand between you and your dreams because of some fleeting experiments that you did not realize would have lasting, detrimental effects on your future.

Experiment carefully and wisely. Check with your mentor first.

Notes

1. Whose image do you admire? Why?

   _____
   _____
   _____

2. What do you need to do to have an image which you can be proud of? Who will help you with those items?

   _____
   _____
   _____

3. What do you do when you are uncertain of the impact of your image? Who do you consult? Who advises you on this matter?

   _____
   _____

4. Do you realize that pictures are forever, even though you may have deleted them?

   _____
   _____

5. What would you do if you have exhibited an image that you later regretted?

   _____
   _____
   _____

6. It is difficult to choose your own image, which differs from that of your friends? How do you do it?

_____
_____
_____

7. How will you learn about appropriate attire for college, job interviews, business attire, and the professional image you need to be successful?

_____
_____
_____

Project

Cut out magazine pictures of professional images that you can visualize for yourself.

Research the attire for your desired career. Cut those images as well.

There's A Queen Within

Reputation

Notes

What are you known for? When you people see you, what do they think? When they think about you, what do they say?

Quiet or wild?

Smart or not into her studies?

Responsible or irresponsible?

Obedient or disobedient?

Respectful or disrespectful?

Defiant or cooperative?

Fearless or flawless?

Predictable or pensive?

Attentive or flighty?

Detailed or high level?

Thinker or speaker?

Serious or fun?

Honest or a liar?

Friend or foe?

Mess-maker or problem solver?

Talker or doer?

Fighter or mediator?

Whatever your reputation is, keep in mind that your reputation is **all** that you have. Many of us have some reputations which we are not proud of and some of the reputations we are very proud of even if we should not be.

Reputation is not something easily restored, so we cannot afford to squander our reputation ever. Our choices need to be smart such that we do not risk our reputation on anything. Recovering from a tarnished reputation is difficult at best.

Reputation is what people think of you based mostly on what you do, and only some of what others say.

Protect you reputation by not being with the wrong crowd or <u>being</u> the wrong crowd. Overcome whatever it is that causes you to want to do the wrong thing.

What will you be remembered for when you go to the ten (10) year high school reunion?

It is a quite the compliment to your character when your classmates talk about how great you were, how they did not invite you to the party because they knew that you did not do drugs or drink alcohol, that the guy of your dreams did not talk to you because he knew that you were not going to have sex, or the "friends" that will not ask you to skip class because they know that your mother would kill you.

Reputation is based on being able to say no to alcohol, drugs, sex, cheating, skipping class, bad behavior, and disrespectful behavior. This is not always easy but you have a future we are working for. Is that temporary situation necessary based on the lasting, detrimental, long-term effects?

Many people around you are considering whether they have enough to live for in order to make the best choice. Some don't. Some don't believe that the hopelessness will ever change.

You need to take the chance that there's hope, enough hope to live past the current situation. Don't squander your future for a temporary thrill.

1. What is a great reputation to you?

___

2. Whose reputation do you admire? Why?

___

3. What is your current reputation? Are you proud of that? Does it need some upgrades?

___

4. What do you want your reputation to be? How will you attain or achieve that reputation? Who can help you achieve that reputation?

___

Project

Put the words together of your ideal reputation in the space below.

Write a letter to your future self about what you are going to do and be as an adult.

Work Ethic

Gage defines work ethic as how well you work and it you are labeled as detailed—oriented versus being labeled as lazy. Work ethic is working hard when you don't feel like it. Work ethic is completing your work, with diligence and with attention to detail. Work ethic is finishing even when it is hard and you don't know everything about your project. Work ethic is doing the work even when you are not sure that it matters.

Do you have work ethic? Do(es) your teacher(s) think that you have work ethic?

Do you know that respect includes work ethic? Getting to class on time, turning in your work on time, and completing that assignment, having given you best effort, and participating at your very best effort are all details of work ethic.

Some of you are or will be athletes. Work ethic includes working on your conditioning by running, practicing, biking, sit-ups, push-ups, and whatever else you need to do to be in shape, so that you can be the best for your team.

Work ethic means that others need to be able to depend on you to do what you are expected to do.

In middle school and high school sports as governed by University Interscholastic League (UIL), if you do not pass your academic classes, then you will not be able to play in the games for your sport(s). Suppose you are the starting player and major point scorer, and you fail a class, you do not have the work ethic that your team needs and deserves.

Work ethic means that you ask for help when you don't know something or just need something.

Work ethic is that you give maximum effort when you feel like it and when you don't. It does not matter how you feel—you work anyway.

Notes

Notes

No matter what others say.

No matter how you feel.

No matter what you are up against.

No matter what you believe.

You still work.

1. Define work ethic.

   _____
   _____
   _____

2. How will you consistently uphold a high work ethic? Who will help you?

   _____
   _____
   _____

3. Who is your work ethic important to? To whom is Your work ethic important?

   _____
   _____
   _____

4. Why is work ethic important?

   _____
   _____
   _____

5. What can you achieve with great work ethic versus if you don't have any work ethic?

   _____
   _____
   _____

6. Who benefits from your work ethic?

_____
_____
_____

7. Whose work ethic do you admire?

_____
_____
_____

8. Does work ethic cost you anything? If so, what?

_____
_____
_____

Project

Pictures of a people with work ethic.

Her Journey to Building Self—Worth

Pictures/words of what you would like to achieve in your life so far.

Integrity

Integrity is synonymous to honesty. Tell the TRUTH! Whew! Really? Tell the whole truth? The real truth? The actual truth?

Integrity is honest in words and deeds and actions. Integrity is a behavior standard. Integrity influences truth. This consideration of integrity means that not only that you are honest, but you act with an increased level of honestly and character.

Integrity means that not only can you be trusted, but you can be counted on to complete a task, carry out the mission of the organization and activity and whatever else you need.

When someone has integrity, it is a step above honesty. It is a compliment. It is an honor. Integrity is your badge of honor.

Integrity is to be protected, because once it is lost then it takes years to recover from that. When you have lied, isn't it true that people don't believe you like they once did? They may put the 'trust but verify' attitude in effect with you. You don't really want people to feel like that about you.

"Lying for no reason."

What is the purpose of lying anyway? The truth will eventually surface. Please remember that google.com is in the palm of the person's hand. Anyone can fact check your story at anytime. Keep in mind that we are people, so sometimes lying delays the consequences but may still surface eventually.

Remember that you want to be viewed as trustworthy and ethical, by everyone, at all times. You do not want to be questioned and disbelieved because you have lied and done some unethical deeds. This is a priority.

Integrity is a part of character, which is what you do when no one is watching. Most people can be great when others are watching, but who are you when no one is watching?

Notes

The other point is what happens when your actions affects the lives and income of other people's lives?

Integrity is a gray area at times, but doing the right thing and for the right reasons is not ever gray.

Tell the truth.

Do the right thing.

Focus on being better.

Be trustworthy.

1. Based on the definition of integrity, what is your definition?

_____
_____
_____

2. How will you use that definition in your everyday life? How will you influence others to do the same?

_____
_____
_____

3. By the definitions and examples, who do you know that has and exercises integrity as an example before you?

_____
_____
_____

4. When have you exercised integrity but it was hard to do the right thing? Give the example.

_____
_____
_____

Project

Make a chart/picture of integrity and 10 synonyms.

Put 10 antonyms on a sticky note for the word integrity.

Her Journey to Building Self—Worth

Challenges/Your Obstacles/Your Past

The easiest thing to do is quit because you have been unsuccessful in your life, by your definition or that of others. I know that if I share with you all of those who have failed, only to realize success one day, one time, you will be amazed, too. What if the persons who created the telephone, electricity, the toilet and indoor plumbing, the computer, the internet, and other things that have been created by people who could have quit—quit?

You are the next _____. You have to fill that blank with your role, job and goals. Because you ARE indeed the next Senator, teacher, chef, custodian, talk show host, President, principal, and all others jobs which exist, and all of those which do not exist yet, which you will invent. You have to prepare for that role, job, and position.

So don't quit! Just like you needed me to do my job by writing this book, be in my place and help you to greatness, you are being counted on as well so you cannot quit. You are permitted a 30 second break to pout or cry or scream, but after that 30 seconds, you resume game on!

Someone needs your gifts to move around in their lives comfortably.

Will greatness cost? Absolutely! But I commit to you that your effort is worth it.

You inspire others with your effort. Use it to fill your journey.

Your obstacles will make you knowledgeable, wiser, and stronger. Keep working towards the goal regardless of the difficulties, that also helps you to be able to appreciate the success you are soon to realize.

Do not continue putting the spotlight on your past. Your past is designed as the foundation of your character. Difficulties help us to know what we <u>are</u> capable of, rather than what we cannot do.

Keep everything in perspective. Trouble does not last always. You will be successful. Don't quit no matter what!

Notes

Notes

I share the best parts of my life with others, even if it was bad because I focus on when I learned from the experience. Further, what will my experience do to help others grow. You should not have to pay for all of those life lessons.

You need guidance and information. Google cannot do everything nor teach you everything. The people, parents, teachers, and mentors, are there to help you with your life, growth, and development.

Your job is to take their experiences and lessons so that you don't have to take that same poor path. You should welcome advice and information which steers you clear of what will harm you. Please consider carefully listening and using the information, rather than rejecting it or discarding it based on your desire to experience life yourself. Keep focused on the end goal of a healthy life, which means that you achieve your dreams and goals with as few obstacles as possible.

Consider what makes life successful and who is doing what you defined as successful. Use what you know to govern your path.

1. What part(s) of your past do you wish would disappear?

_____
_____
_____

2. What would you change about your current life? Why? How can you make some changes so that your life could resemble what you wish that it would look like?

_____
_____
_____

3. Are you proud of your family? Surroundings? Legacy?

_____
_____
_____

4. What will be different about your life because of your past and present?

_____
_____
_____

5. Who helps you make these changes and adjustments?

_____
_____

Project

Forgiveness Letters: Write 3 letters to persons who have harmed you, starting with yourself.

I forgive me.

I forgive _____.

Her Journey to Building Self—Worth

I forgive _____.

Love letters.

Write letters to yourself and two other people.

I love myself, or at least I am learning to love myself.

___

Love letter to _____ .

Love letter to _____.

Her Journey to Building Self—Worth

ONEDIA N. GAGE, PH. D.

Future

What does your future hold? No one knows exactly. Some people will do exactly what they dreamed of as a child, while others will do something very different. Whatever you do with your future, remember that certain 'today' and 'right now' choices can stall your future.

My daughter got her first job at 15 years old and she had to take a drug test. What if she had been involved in drugs? She would not be eligible to work.

Any drug conviction will lead to your ineligibility for federal student aid. On the financial aid student report form (fafsa.gov), there is a question about drug conviction. Then there is a database connected to the drug related to convictions, so even if you lie, you will be denied financial aid. How then will you be able to attend college?

Drugs should not be a part of today because it changes tomorrow.

Sex should be omitted because pregnancy or disease can impact tomorrow. Some people have a good enough support base to raise your child while you attend college, but most do not.

Your future is determined by your today. Choose wisely.

Don't think that you will never get caught.

Don't think that it will never happen to you.

Your future is worth waiting for and even saying no.

Is your future worth a small moment to risk that experiment? I do not think so.

Dream the Best of Dreams

Dream the best of dreams, not what the people or your surroundings limit you to.

Notes

I always wanted to go to Stanford University. My mother told me no. I tried to obey and I did not go. Shortly after I graduated, we did not really have the relationship for which I hoped. I never made it to California like I wanted to though. I have visited. She and I still don't have a relationship that a mother and daughter should have. If we were going to have the same relationship as if I had defied her, I should have gone to California.

I am not saying to defy your parents. I am saying consider your dreams and pursue them with all that you are.

Don't let anyone stop you.

Research your desires. Don't listen without checking the facts.

Plan a great life.

Live it!

1. What do you want to be in the future? What education is required for that job? Who do you know that has done that job/career?

___

2. Where do you want to live when you grow up? What does housing cost in that area? What does your salary need to be to live there?

___

3. Who will you mentor? Who will you share your insight with so that she will achieve more than others believe possible?

___

4. What grades do you need to earn in high school to be accepted into the college of your dreams? Are you on track to achieve that? If not, what do you need to change?

___

5. Do you need help achieving your goals? Who will you ask?

_____
_____
_____

6. What will you do to overcome any obstacles you will face? How will you manage your motivation when you reach obstacles?

_____
_____
_____

Project

Vision Board: Creation and Completion

A vision board is a visualization tool which refers to a board of any sort used to build a collage of words and pictures that represent your goals and dreams.

https://www.makeavisionboard.com/what-is-a-vision-board/

Items needed for a vision board: glue, poster board, magazine pictures.

Elements for a vision board: goals, places, dreams.

Use the next two pages to create the Board.

Vision Board

Vision Board

Vision Board Narrative

Vision Board Narrative

Reflection

Reflection

Her Journey to Building Self—Worth

Appendix

Goals — 122
    How to create them
    How to reach them

Mission — 124

Vision — 127

Values — 131

Dreams — 133

Goals

goal [gohl] *noun*

the result or achievement toward which effort is directed; aim; end.

The questions that you answer when developing goals are as follows:

1. What do I want to accomplish?
2. When do I want to accomplish this by?
3. Who is going to help me and hold me accountable?
4. What do you do when you do not meet the goals as planned?
5. Who do you share your successes with?

Goals

Goals   **By When**   **Who**

Mission Statement

A personal mission statement is based on habit 2 of <u>7 Habits of Highly Effective People</u> called begin with the end in mind. In ones life, the most effective way to begin with the end in mind is to develop a mission statement one that focuses what you want to be in terms of character and what you want to do in reference to contribution of achievements. Writing a mission statement can be the most important activity an individual can take to truly lead ones life.

Victor Hugo once said there is nothing as powerful as an idea whose time has finally come, you may call it a credo, a philosophy, you may call it a purpose statement, it's not as important as to what you call it, no it's how you define your definition. That mission and vision statement is more powerful more significant, more influential, than the baggage of the past, or even the accumulated noise of the present.

What is a mission statement you ask? Personal mission statements based on correct principles are like a personal constitution, the basis for making major, life-directing decisions, the basis for making daily decisions in the midst of the circumstances and emotions that affect our lives.

Your statement may be a few words or several pages, but it is not a "to do" list. It reflects your uniqueness and must speak to you powerfully about the person you are and the person you are becoming.

Why should you write a personal mission statement?

Numerous experts on leadership and personal development emphasize how vital it is for you to craft your own personal vision for your life. Warren Bennis, Stephen Covey, Peter Senge, and others point out that a powerful vision can help you succeed far beyond where you'd be without one. That vision can propel you and inspire those around you to reach their own dreams.

Q: How do I go about creating my Personal Mission Statement?

A: A Mission Statement is defined as having goals and a deadline. This is opposed to the notion that a Mission Statement is just a bunch of flowery, general phrases like, "I will be the best business person I can be."

What should you include when writing a great personal mission statement?

- describe your best characteristics and how you express them
- have specific, measurable outcomes (or goals)

- have a deadline — for example, December 31st 2012, or a year from today.

When Stephen Covey talks about 'mission statement' in this quote he is referring to the articulation of your life purpose. "If you don't set your goals based upon your Mission Statement, you may be climbing the ladder of success only to realize, when you get to the top, you're on the WRONG BUILDING." **Stephen Covey – 7 Habits of Highly Effective People.**

Mission Statement Example – Poor (It's more like a Vision Statement)

"I aspire to start my own business. I want to help others and be a better businesswoman. I will deliver the best food with the highest service levels." Jane

Mission Statement Example – Better

"I will start my business within 3 months and plan to grow it to $500,000 in revenues within a year. Using this success my staff and I will spread the word to local schools and businesses about eco-friendly food production in order that we reach at least 100 people within the same time frame. My purpose will be to massively add value to our local community in measurable ways that have a real impact on people's health now and in the future" Jane

What to do with your Mission Statement?

So now we have a mission we can set a range of goals on the road to achieving your outcomes and dreams. Your values are clarified and should be in line with the goals you want to achieve in life so you should find it easier to make decisions and to do the "right thing" because you can simply ask yourself, "Will this help me achieve my mission?"

You can even put your mission statement in an area where your family or even co-workers will see it. For, a mission statement defines who you are and what you stand for. This lets people see how you think and feel, which in turn, will help them respect, think and act in line with your values too.

Mission Statement

Vision Statement

A personal vision/mission statement is the framework for creating a powerful life.

Your personal vision statement provides the direction necessary to guide the course of your days and the choices you make about your life.

The idea is to craft a broad based idea about your life and what will really make it exciting and fulfilling, that's your life vision.

From the vision, you craft a more focused and action orientated "mission" statement based on "purpose". And finally you get to a list of goals, wishes, desires and needs.

In his book 'The Success Principles', Jack Canfield tells us that in order to create a balanced and successful life; your vision needs to include the following seven areas:

1. work and career
2. finances
3. recreation and free time
4. health and fitness
5. relationships
6. personal goals
7. contribution to the larger community

It does not include the distinctive ways that you intend to accomplish your purpose.

Why Write a Personal Vision Statement?

To express:

- your purpose
- your life's dream
- your core values & beliefs
- what you want for yourself
- what you want to contribute to others
- what you want to be

Characteristics of a Vision Statement:

- Engages your heart & spirit
- Taps into embedded concerns & needs
- Asserts what you want to create
- Is something worth going for
- Provides meaning to the work you do
- Is a little cloudy and grand
- Is simple
- Is a living document
- Provides a starting place from which to get more specificity
- Is based on quality and dedication

Key Elements of a Vision Statement:

- Written down and referred to daily
- Written in present tense, as if it has already been completed
- Includes a variety of activities and time frames
- Filled with descriptive details that anchor it to reality

What Visions Are Not:

- A mission statement: "Why do we exist now?"
- A strategic plan: "How do we plan to get there?"
- A set of objectives: "We will accomplish X by Y time to Z% target audience."

Use these questions to guide your thoughts:

- What are the ten things you most enjoy doing? Be honest. These are the ten things without which your weeks, months, and years would feel incomplete.
- What three things must you do every single day to feel fulfilled in your work?
- What are your five-six most important values?
- Your life has a number of important facets or dimensions, all of which deserve some attention in your personal vision statement.
- Write one important goal for each of them: physical, spiritual, work or career, family, social relationships, financial security, mental improvement and attention, and fun.
- If you never had to work another day in your life, how would you spend your time instead of working?

- When your life is ending, what will you regret not doing, seeing, or achieving?
- What strengths have other people commented on about you and your accomplishments? What strengths do you see in yourself?

Vision Statement

Values Statement

A personal **value** is absolute or relative and ethical value, the assumption of which can be the basis for ethical action. A *value system* is a set of consistent values and measures. A *principle value* is a foundation upon which other values and measures of integrity are based.

Some values are physiologically determined and are normally considered objective, such as a desire to avoid physical pain or to seek pleasure. Other values are considered subjective, vary across individuals and cultures, and are in many ways aligned with belief and belief systems. Types of values include ethical/moral values, doctrinal/ideological (religious, political) values, social values, and aesthetic values. It is debated whether some values that are not clearly physiologically determined, such as altruism, are intrinsic, and whether some, such as acquisitiveness, should be classified as vices or virtues. Values have been studied in various disciplines: anthropology, behavioral economics, business ethics, corporate governance, moral philosophy, political sciences, social psychology, sociology and theology to name a few.

Values can be defined as broad preference concerning appropriate courses of action or outcomes. As such, values reflect a person's sense of right and wrong or what "ought" to be. "Equal rights for all", "Excellence deserves admiration", and "People should be treated with respect and dignity" are representative of values. Values tend to influence attitudes and behavior.

Values Statement

Dreams List

Resources

http://www.usa.gov/Topics/Teens.shtml

http://www.teenink.com/Resources

http://www.parentandteenresources.com/

http://www.hhs.gov/ash/oah/oah-initiatives/teen_pregnancy/

http://www.cdc.gov/teenpregnancy/parents.htm

www.thenationalcampaign.org/resources/

http://www.suicidepreventionlifeline.org/

http://www.drugfree.org/

http://kidshealth.org/teen/food_fitness/dieting/obesity.html

http://www.medicalnewstoday.com/articles/268983.php

http://www.jhsph.edu/research/centers-and-institutes/center-for-adolescent-health/_includes/Obesity_Standalone.pdf

www.agirlsday.org

www.mymotherdaughter.com

www.onediagagespeaks.com

www.girlsinc.org

www.haul.org

The Five Love Languages for Teens by Gary Chapman

Acknowledgments

God, thank You for Your plans for me. Thank You for **There is a Queen Within: Her Journey to Building Self—Worth** and choosing me to complete Your project. I just want to please You. Thank You for continuing to anoint me and to invest in me and my gifts, which keep surprising me. Thank You for loving and forgiving me.

Thank you Adrienne Henderson for reading this work and offering your feedback. Hopefully, this work will change lives and extend our work such that girls everywhere will be able to grow into the beautiful women they are designed to be.

Hillary and Nehemiah, thank you for supporting me and my endeavors. Thank you for loving me, especially when I do nothing without a pen and a clipboard, thank you for enduring my late nights, your ideas, the sounding board, the love and the support. Thank you for celebrating our legacy.

To the girls who have raised their hands in need of these lessons. I don't know all of you, but to the ones I do know, I apologize. I got it to you as quickly as I could. I love you!

To my prayer partners and to my accountability partners, thank you for the long talks and the powerful prayers and the encouragement. To my pastor and church family, thank you so much for your love and support.

Her Journey to Building Self—Worth

Onedia N. Gage, Ph. D., seeks to share her outlandish pursuit of education and value for girls with all who need to enhance her self-esteem. Please seek your authentic self. Gage is a true advocate for all girls. As a girl who had a few advocates, she still could have used more. Still needs one now.

Please feel free to contact her.
onediagage@onediagagespeaks.com, or
@onediangage (twitter). www.onediagagespeaks.com

Blogtalkradio.com/onediagage

Youtube.com/onediagage10

Facebook.com/onedia-gage

Her Journey to Building Self—Worth

ADVOCATE ♦ TEACHER ♦ FACILITATOR

CONFERENCE SPEAKER ♦ WORKSHOP LEADER

To invite Dr. Onedia Gage to speak to the teens at your school or organization,

Please contact us at: www.onediagespeaks.com

@onediangage (twitter) ♦ onediagage@onediagespeaks.com ♦ facebook.com/onediagage
youtube.com/onediagage10 ♦ blogtalkradio.com/onediagage ♦ ongage (Instagram)

Publishing

Do you have a book you want to write, but do not know what to do?
Do you have a book you need to publish but do not know how to start?
Would publishing move your career forward?

Let us help

onediagage@purpleink.net ♦ www.purpleink.net

281.740.5143 ♦ 713.705.5530

www.ingramcontent.com/pod-product-compliance
Lightning Source LLC
Chambersburg PA
CBHW081749100526
44592CB00015B/2352